The Secret In Our Genes:
Out Of Africa
And Into The World:
Unlocking Hidden Histories
Embedded in Our DNA

BUELO ADDAEYAH
AFIA HENEWAA

Copyright © 2025 FeNIIX Publishing

No part of this book may be reproduced, distributed, or
transmitted in any form or by any means, including photocopying,
recording, or other electronic or mechanical methods, without the prior
written permission of the author, except in the case of brief quotations
embodied in critical reviews, educational uses, or other noncommercial uses
permitted by copyright law.

All rights to cited works belong to their respective owners and are
used here under the doctrine of fair use or with express permission.

All rights reserved.

ISBN: 9798218620370

DEDICATION

To the loving memory of my mother, **Florene**, whose Mende roots run deep within my own, grounding me in heritage, resilience, and love. And to the cherished memory of her twin sister, my beloved **Aunt Clorene**, who, with her *'Little Black Book'* of family members, connected us across oceans and borders, from Puerto Rico, Tortola, the Virgin Islands, and throughout the U.S. Together, you were the pillars of our family's legacy. Forever hold a place for me in our ancestor's realm.

To the loving memory of my beloved grandmothers, **Reba** and **Leola.**

Thank you for having "Grandma's Hands." Your hands did more than hold us—they were symbols of love, resilience, and wisdom that shaped our lives. They worked tirelessly, often behind the scenes, to ensure that everyone was cared for, teaching by example the meaning of strength, humility, and grace. Your hands prepared meals from scratch, tended to gardens, rocked children to sleep, and lifted us in moments of joy and sorrow. Through every gentle touch and firm guidance, you passed down courage, selflessness, and the stories that kept our family grounded.

In loving memory of my **Uncle *"mi Tio"* Stanley** and **Aunt Rita**, and to **Aunt Macy**, whose presence still blesses us, for their dedication to preserving the deep knowledge of our family ties and history across the U.S., Puerto Rico, Tortola, and the Virgin Islands, which inspired the creation of the next generation's little black book, *'Williams' List.'* Their dedication to preserving our stories fueled our connection to one another and to our past.

To Cousins **Pearle**, **Christophena**, and **Myrtle**, the *cotton fabric* and Ancestral Matriarchs of our family, you are the essential threads that hold the family together. You represent something foundational, warm, and strong, tying back to history and tradition. You are the everyday material—reliable, comforting, and woven through each generation—keeping stories, connections, and traditions alive in a practical, lasting way. Your stories and memories are like fibers that, when woven together, form a fabric that connects the past with the present.

BUELO ADDAEYAH | AFIA HENEWAA

CONTENTS

	Acknowledgments	i
1	The Gift of Heritage	Pg 7
2	The Neolithic Ancestors of Southeast Africa	Pg 10
3	The Great Bantu Migration	Pg 12
4	The Pharaoh Connection – Ties to Ancient Egypt	Pg 13
5	The Hebrew Israelites – Tribe of Judah	Pg 14
6	West and Central African Heritage	Pg 22
7	The Mandinka and Balanta Legacy	Pg 26
8	Taken: The Perilous Journey to the Americas	Pg 29
9	Cultural Resilience Through the African Diaspora	Pg 33
10	Honoring Ancestry and Heritage	Pg 36

ACKNOWLEDGMENTS

This book is a tribute to the journey and resilience of my ancestors, who lived, thrived, and passed down a legacy that I am privileged to carry forward. To my family, whose stories and histories inspire me daily—thank you for your love, encouragement, and for always reminding me of the importance of our heritage.

A heartfelt Thank you to my wife, Zoa, "Afia Henewaa," for your unwavering support, love, and wisdom. You are my foundation and strength, and the one who makes everything possible. Your editorial expertise and thoughtful insights have greatly enriched this book, and your belief in this project and in me has been a constant source of motivation. Thank you for helping bring this vision to life.

To our children—BJ and his wife, Candace, who gave us our three beautiful granddaughters, and Alphonso, Edward, Johnt'e, Tyra, and Ellis—thank you for being the heart of our family. Your love, strength, and joy inspire us daily to honor our heritage and pass down our stories. This journey and this book are dedicated to you, with deep gratitude for the role you play in keeping our family's legacy alive.

To our granddaughters, Ariella (11), Gabriella (5), and Isabella (4), whose boundless curiosity and joy make storytelling a delight—you are the reason I am passionate about preserving our family's legacy. I am grateful to you for the questions you ask, the wonder you bring, and the love you hold for learning about where we come from. You are my constant inspiration and the future I write for.

Finally, a special thanks to the researchers, historians, and genealogists who have helped illuminate the path back through the generations, connecting me with pieces of our family's story. Your dedication to uncovering the truth about our shared history, across continents and cultures, is invaluable.

1 THE GIFT OF HERITAGE

Our family's story began a long time ago in lands far away. From the wide, open plains of Africa (Alkebulan) to the great river called the Nile, our ancestors explored, built, and created amazing things that still inspire us today. This book will take you on a journey through our family's roots—from the ancient lands of Southeast and West Africa, to the powerful kingdoms of Egypt, and all the way to a place in Northeast Africa, now called the Middle East. These roots are the beginning of who we are, living in our hearts and connecting us to those who came before us. Let's discover the incredible history that makes us who we are!

For Illustration Purposes Only. Map of Africa with ancient roots marked in flowing lines, connecting various regions.

Long ago, our ancestors lived in amazing places full of beauty and special traditions. They made their homes near tall mountains, busy trade routes, and quiet villages under the stars. In these places, they worked hard, dreamed big, and grew strong, carrying stories and wisdom that have lasted through the ages. With open skies above them and rich land beneath them, they shared knowledge and traveled, building connections with people and places across Africa. Today, we honor their stories and remember their strength and courage, which have shaped our family for so many years.

Imagine traveling back thousands of years to places filled with wide-open lands, powerful kingdoms, and long-lasting traditions. Our ancestors lived in areas we now call The Great Rift Valley, which includes Israel, Kenya, Tanzania, Mozambique, and Malawi. Some moved to West Africa, settling in places like Senegal, The Gambia, Guinea, Sierra Leone, Liberia, Ghana, Nigeria, and the Congo. Others lived in North Africa, in Egypt, and in areas near the Middle East (Levant), where they became part of the history of the Pharaohs in Egypt and the Tribe of Judah in Yasharal (Israel).

For Illustration Purposes Only. A heartwarming depiction of Buelo reading to Ariella, Gabriella, and Isabella about their proud ancestral family heritage.

One quiet evening, Buelo sat with his three granddaughters—Ariella, Gabriella, and Isabella. Smiling, he said, "Tonight, I have a special story to share. It's the story of where we come from."

Isabella looked up with wide eyes. "Where *did* our family come from?"

Buelo chuckled and set down his cup. "That's a great question, Isabella," he said warmly. "Our family's journey began a long time ago, in places full of beautiful landscapes and powerful kingdoms. Our ancestors lived in lands rich with stories, people, and traditions. And our 'Gene Code'—what I like to call *Discovery, Nature, and Ancestors* (DNA)—still helps shape who we are today."

"DNA is like the recipe book for your whole body. It's inside every cell — like a tiny instruction manual — and it tells your body what color your eyes are, how your hair curls, how tall you might grow, and even how your skin protects you. You got your DNA from your parents, and they got theirs from their parents — all the way back through history. That's how you're connected to our ancestors. It's like having a time-travel map inside your body that tells the story of where you come from. So every time you smile, dance, speak, or even just breathe — your DNA is helping you do it, and it's doing it with a little piece of everyone who came before you."

2 THE NEOLITHIC ANCESTORS OF SOUTHEAST AFRICA

Our family's roots go back to the very beginning of human history in Southeast Africa. Our ancestors were some of the first people to grow crops, build homes, and live in harmony with nature. They were part of early communities from around 10,000 years ago, working together, and taking care of the land. These early families paved the way for many generations to come.

For Illustration Purposes Only. A peaceful village in Southeast Africa, with people working the land and children playing.

They lived simple, peaceful lives, growing food and taking care of animals. They passed their knowledge down to their children, staying closely connected to the earth and their surroundings.

Gabriella looked up with bright curiosity. "Buelo, what would I be doing if I lived a long, long time ago in those times?"

Buelo chuckled, picturing his little granddaughter in that ancient world. "Well, Gabby," he said, "you'd probably be a great helper! You might go with your family to gather berries, nuts, and plants, learning which ones were good to eat. Maybe you'd help take care of the animals, feeding them and keeping an eye on them. And in the evenings, you'd sit around the fire, listening to stories and watching your family make tools and pottery. You'd be learning and playing every day, just like now, but spending lots of time outside!"

Gabriella's eyes sparkled as she imagined herself in a world of open fields and warm fires, helping her family and exploring the land.

For Illustration Purposes Only. An elder ancestor gathers the tribe around a fire for oral history lessons; passing down the legacy of their people for generations to come.

Ariella leaned in, not wanting to miss out, and asked, "Buelo, what kinds of traditions would we have back then?"

Buelo smiled, happy with her thoughtful question. "Ari, traditions were very important to our ancestors. Families would come together for special events, like celebrating the changing seasons or the harvest. They'd play music with drums, sing songs that had been passed down, and tell stories around the fire—stories about courage, wisdom, and the beauty of the earth. You'd probably learn how to dance to the drumbeats and help make special meals, learning all the family recipes by heart."

3 THE GREAT BANTU MIGRATION

As time went on, our ancestors became part of one of the biggest movements in African history—the Bantu migration. This wasn't just about moving to new places; it was about sharing culture, language, and traditions. The Bantu-speaking people traveled all across Africa, teaching others how to farm, work with metals, and speak new languages.

Our ancestors traveled with the Bantu people, finding new lands and building homes in places full of resources. As they moved, they met new people and learned about their cultures, but they always kept their own traditions and the wisdom passed down from their ancestors."

For Illustration Purposes Only. African Bantu families journeying across open plains, carrying their belongings and guiding livestock, while trading goods and ideas along the way.

Isabella looked up and asked, "Buelo, what's a migration?"

Buelo smiled warmly. "A migration is when people, animals, or even birds move to a new place to live. Our ancestors moved to find warmer places or land to grow food. Their journey is a big part of our story, too!"

4 THE PHARAOH CONNECTION – TIES TO ANCIENT EGYPT

For Illustration Purposes Only. Pharaoh Ramesses III in full royal attire, including a ceremonial headdress.

For Illustration Purposes Only. A map of Egypt, showing its key cities, the Nile River, and trade routes connecting Egypt with the surrounding regions.

Our journey continues to North Africa, to the land of Egypt (also called Kemet or Mitzrayim). Ancient Egypt was one of the greatest civilizations in history and an important part of our family's story. Our family is connected to Pharaoh Ramesses III, a powerful leader from ancient Egypt's 20th Dynasty, which was over 3,000 years ago! He protected Egypt from invaders and ruled with wisdom.

Egypt has deep roots in African culture and history. The ancient Egyptians were not just people of the Nile—they were Africans who helped shape the ancient world. Their stories of kings, gods, and everyday life are now part of our family's legacy.

5 THE HEBREW ISRAELITES – TRIBE OF JUDAH

Our family's story is connected to Africa through the Bantu people of Southeast and West Africa and to North Africa through Pharaoh Ramesses III of ancient Egypt. But there's another special part of our story that leads us to the Hebrew Israelites; specifically, the Tribe of Judah.

Six ancestors—we'll call Necha, Hila, Sorril, Eliyashiv, Ishbod, and Berel—lived in ancient Israel a long, long time ago, from about 8030 BC to 3050 BC. They were part of the Tribe of Judah, one of the 12 tribes of Israel, and their lives were part of

For Illustration Purposes Only. An ancient depiction of young Hebrew Israelite children from the Tribe of Judah playing together in an outdoor courtyard with stone structures and ancient architecture, wearing traditional robes and head coverings reflective of ancient times. The children are joyfully engaging in games, capturing a sense of community, laughter, and friendship in a warm, sunlit setting.

the ancient Israelite story. This connection is another important piece of our family's amazing history.

The Tribe of Judah is very special in the Bible, known for its brave warriors, wise leaders, and being part of King David's family line. We are connected to this strong and proud tribe, which stands for strength, resilience, and a history that shaped the Hebrew people.

Gabriella looked at Buelo with curiosity and asked, "What did Israelite kids play with back then?"

Buelo chuckled softly, imagining the times of the Hebrew Israelites. "Well, Gabby, kids back then didn't have the toys we have today, but they still found ways to have fun. They made their own toys from things around them—like stones, clay, sticks, or animal skins. Some kids made little figurines, and others played games where they ran, jumped, and pretended to be heroes or warriors."

For Illustration Purposes Only. King David from the Hebrew Israelites Tribe of Judah, wearing fringed robes and a head covering with symbolic patterns, surrounded by elements of Hebrew culture.

Buelo smiled, thinking about how creative children were. "They also played games that helped them learn important skills, like how to throw a sling or take care of animals, just like their parents. Their games taught them how to be strong, smart, and ready for the future—just like you learn when you play today."

The Story of Necha – נֶחָה

For Illustration Purposes Only. A depiction of Necha, a young Hebrew ancestor from around 3050 BC, crafting bronze and copper bowls in Bethlehem. She is shown in an outdoor setting with rolling hills and ancient paths in the background, wearing a traditional linen garment with a waist sash, and intricate jewelry.

My name is Necha, which means "Comfort," and I lived in Bethlehem around 3050 BC. Bethlehem is a busy and lively place, full of stories, culture, and strong people. Our city, nestled in the Judean hills, is where many travelers pass through. People come from faraway lands like Egypt, Jaffa, and Mesopotamia, sharing stories about their journeys and the customs they follow. The King's Highway, a famous trade route, brings travelers and merchants to our city, filling our days with new faces, languages, and goods.

I spend my days in a workshop, making bronze and copper bowls for our village. Making these bowls is a special tradition I learned from my elders. They taught me that every creation carries the spirit of the person who made it. To me, each bowl is more than just metal—it holds blessings and stories. As I shape and polish the bowls, I think about the tales travelers share—of rivers, shining temples, and their customs. These stories inspire the patterns I create.

When merchants and wanderers visit Bethlehem, they admire the bowls I make. They touch them gently and say, "This bowl carries the strength of its maker." I smile, proud that each piece I make holds part of our city's story and reflects the journeys of those who pass through.

The Story of Hila – הִילָה

For Illustration Purposes Only. A young Hebrew ancestor named Hila sitting and making beads. She is wearing traditional attire, including a modest robe with vibrant patterns and a head covering. Hila is focused on her craft, stringing colorful beads, with a collection of beads and making tools around her. The setting is simple and warm, emphasizing her creativity and dedication to bead-making, with sunlight streaming gently through a nearby natural opening.

My name is Hila, which means "Halo" or "Crown," and I lived near what is now called Hebron around 3050 BC. Our city, high in the Judean Mountains, is surrounded by strong walls for protection. Some nomadic tribes still pass through the area, but not as many as before. Our ruler sends tribute, or gifts, to the Pharaoh of Egypt, and in return, the Pharaoh helps us when there's trouble with other tribes. The King's Highway, a famous trade route, brings merchants to our city, where we sell our goods and learn about faraway places.

I am known for making glass bead jewelry. The beads, brought by merchants from distant lands, shimmer like stars and are loved by everyone who sees them. When I hold the beads, I think about the stories they carry—where they came from and the journeys they've taken. My jewelry connects us all, just like the stars in the sky.

I fell in love with bead-making, watching my mother and grandmother string beads under the soft light of our home. The beads, brought by brave traders traveling the King's Highway, were more than just decorations—they were treasures from faraway lands. I learned the techniques my family passed down, carefully shaping and polishing each bead. As I grew, my skills improved, and soon my jewelry was worn not only by my family but also by travelers, nobles, and even important visitors to our city.

The Story of Sorril – סוֹרִיל

For Illustration Purposes Only. A depiction of Sorril, a Hebrew ancestor living in Lachish, Israel, set within a calm village nestled by the Judean mountains. Sorril wears traditional clothing adorned with cultural patterns. Her attire includes a headscarf wrapped elegantly around her head. The village features stone houses surrounded by olive trees and terraced hills.

My name is Sorril, which means "Warmth," and I lived in Lachish around 8050 BC. Our village is peaceful, nestled by the Judean mountains. Life here follows the natural rhythms of the land and the traditions of our people. I have a special role as the Keeper of Traditions. It is my job to remember and share the stories, wisdom, and practices that keep our community connected.

I guide rituals to celebrate the changing seasons, lead songs and prayers during gatherings, and teach others about herbs, healing, and crafts. People come to me for advice because they trust my calm and thoughtful words. The children love sitting with me to hear stories about our ancestors and how they lived in harmony with the earth. When there are disagreements, I help bring peace by reminding everyone of the strong bonds we share.

I often say, "To know who we are, we must remember where we come from. Our traditions are a thread that ties the past, present, and future together. Through our steps on this soil and the stories we share, we honor all who came before us and all who will come after."

The Story of Eliyashiv – אֶלְיָשִׁיב

For Illustration Purposes Only: Eliyashiv, standing on a hill overlooking the fortified city. The city, constructed with mudbrick walls, is set at the edge of the Negev Desert where desert sands meet fertile plains. Eliyashiv wears traditional desert attire, and carries a spear tipped with obsidian (sharp volcanic glass). He is youthful, with a focused expression and a hint of pride, signifying resilience. The background shows Arad's buildings and agriculture, with goats and sheep grazing nearby. The King's Highway stretches in the distance. The sky is painted with a warm desert sunset, emphasizing a sense of endurance and community strength.

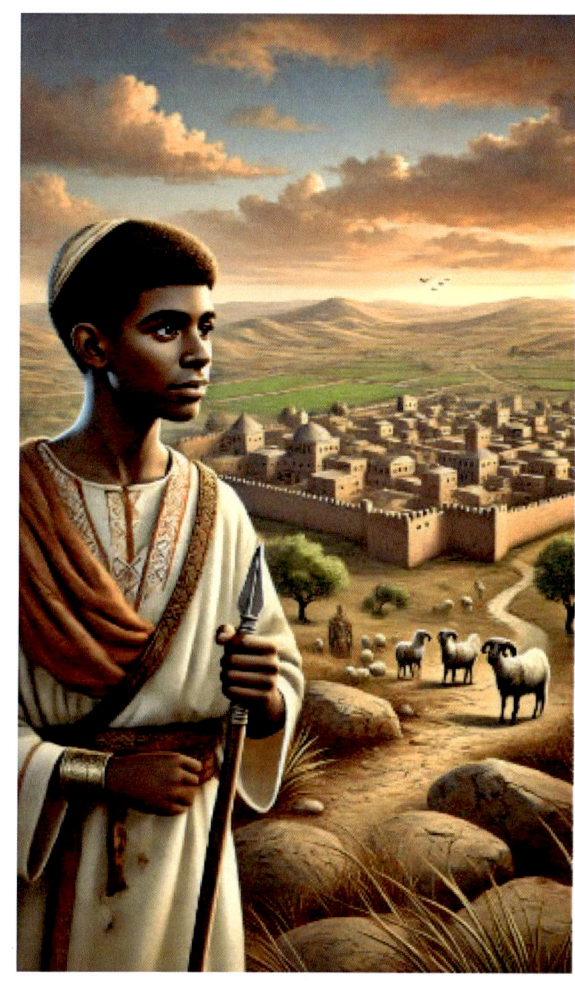

My name is Eliyashiv, which means "God has restored," and I lived in Arad, a city on the edge of the Negev Desert, around 3050 BC. Arad is a strong and safe place, built on a hill with mudbrick walls to protect us from raiders and wild animals. Life here can be hard, but we have learned to thrive in the land where the desert meets fertile plains.

The Negev is not empty—it has many hidden resources. We collect water from underground reservoirs, which help us through the dry seasons. Our people grow barley, wheat, and olives in the fertile land around the city. We also raise goats and sheep, which give us milk, meat, and wool to use and trade.

The King's Highway, a famous trade route, passes close to our city. Traders bring copper from Sinai, turquoise from Egypt, and spices from Arabia. In return, we trade wool, olive oil, and pottery made by our artists. My father is a trader, and I often go with him on journeys to meet people from other cities. These trips show me how big and amazing the world is, filled with different people and their ways of life.

The Story of Ishbod – אִישָׁבוֹד

For Illustration Purposes Only: A depiction of Ishbod, a Hebrew ancestor from Lachish in ancient Canaan. He is standing proudly, surrounded by cattle and horses, which he raises to trade along the Via Maris trade route. He wears traditional garments made of simple, woven cloth, with a hint of ruggedness from his work. The landscape around him is open and warm, showing the lowlands with hints of the Judean mountains in the background.

My name is Ishbod, which means "Glory." I lived in Lachish, a city near the Judean mountains, around 3050 BC. Our city is close to the Mediterranean Sea, just a day's walk away. On special occasions, we travel there to meet merchants on the Via Maris (way of the sea) trade route. This road connects Egypt to faraway places like Syria, Mesopotamia, and Anatolia.

The cities along this route are huge, with tall walls that protect their people and treasures. At these marketplaces, we meet traders who bring fine pottery, copper tools, and rare oils. They come to us for strong cattle and sturdy horses, which I help raise and care for. My father taught me how to take care of the animals, showing me how to breed the strongest ones to trade with merchants.

In the evenings, my family and I gather around the fire to share stories. We talk about faraway lands, rivers beyond mountains, and cities so tall they touch the sky. The merchants tell us about their travels, using stars to guide them and the strange places they've seen. When they look at our cattle, they see livestock. But when I look at them, I see my family's pride and the part we play in connecting people and cultures across the ancient world.

The Story of Berel – בֶּרִיל

For Illustration Purposes Only. Berel, a Hebrew ancestor, standing confidently in a rugged landscape near Hebron. The background features rolling hills and wild vegetation. Berel holds a sharp-tipped spear made from stone, with a strong wooden shaft. He wears simple attire made of animal hides and woven fabric, suited for a hunter-gatherer lifestyle. His expression is determined yet thoughtful, reflecting his role as a protector of his community. The scene emphasizes his connection to nature and his readiness to defend his people.

My name is Berel, which means "Bear." I lived near Hebron, around 8050 BC, in what will one day be called the Judean Mountains. Our community is small, but we often meet nomads (wanderers) passing through the hills and valleys. They don't stay long, but we share the land and sometimes learn from each other.

Unlike the big cities far to the north, we do not need strong walls. Our main concern is protecting our sheep and goats from wild animals like wolves, leopards, and even lions. We watch over our herds carefully, using spears and arrows to keep predators away.

We depend on the land for everything. We grow wheat in the fields, but when the harvest isn't enough, we gather wild grains, berries, nuts, and fruits from the forests and hills. Underground tunnels help us store food for tougher times, and we use stone tools we make ourselves to dig them out.

Hunting is also very important. With sharp spears and arrows, we work together to track and bring down large animals. Hunting takes teamwork, patience, and respect for the life we take. The meat feeds our families, the hides keep us warm, and the bones are turned into tools or ornaments to use and share.

6 WEST AND CENTRAL AFRICAN HERITAGE

For Illustration Purposes Only. A depiction of Yoruba children in Nigeria, engaging in traditional play and activities in a village setting. The children wear colorful traditional attire, including brightly patterned clothing such as buba (robe) and wrappers (long skirt). Some children are playing a game similar to ayo (a traditional African board game), while others run and chase each other joyfully. The setting includes traditional huts and a backdrop of lush greenery, with a sense of community warmth and cultural pride evident in their expressions and interactions.

In the warm glow of the evening, Buelo leaned back in his chair, his hands resting on its arms as he listened to the eager questions of Ariella, Gabriella, and Isabella. A map spread out on the table seemed almost alive, with lines and colors showing the story of their ancestry. The room was full of curiosity.

"Buelo," Ariella began, her voice soft but full of wonder, "you've told us about Southeast Africa, Egypt, and Israel, but what about the rest of Africa? Are we connected to other places too?"

Buelo smiled warmly, his eyes sparkling with pride. "That's such a great question, Ari," he said, leaning forward and tracing the map with his finger. "Yes, our roots stretch far and wide across Africa. A big part of our heritage comes from West and Central Africa—lands full of incredible stories, kingdoms, and cultures that shaped not only us but the world."

He paused, pointing to the curve of Africa's western coast. "Let's start with Nigeria," he said. "This is the land of the Yoruba, Igbo, and Hausa-Fulani peoples—some of the most amazing cultures in history. The Yoruba are known for their deep spiritual beliefs, especially the Orishas, who are like guides. They believed the Orishas gave them wisdom and courage and even helped them with everyday things, like planting crops or creating art. Did you know their drummers could send messages between villages just by using rhythms? It's like they had their own secret language!"

For Illustration Purposes Only. A depiction of the Igbo people of Nigeria, featuring men, women, and children in a village scene. The men wear isiagu tops with red caps (okpu agu), and the women are adorned in colorful traditional attire, including wrappers, blouses, and headwraps. The scene shows community activities such as a traditional dance with musicians playing instruments like drums and flutes. The background has traditional Igbo huts, palm trees, and a lively atmosphere, highlighting their vibrant culture and unity.

"The Igbo are known for being creative and smart," Buelo continued. "They made market systems that are still studied today! Their masquerades are colorful, lively performances that celebrate life, death, and everything in between. And the Hausa-Fulani? They were amazing traders, scholars, and rulers who built cities that became important places for learning and trade."

Gabriella tilted her head thoughtfully. "Buelo, what about Ghana or Sierra Leone? Did our family come from there too?"

Buelo smiled and nodded, moving his finger across the map. "Yes, Gabby. Ghana, home to the Akan people, had powerful kingdoms like the Ashanti Empire. These kingdoms were built on gold, wisdom, and strength. You know the colorful kente cloth we sometimes see at ceremonies? Each color and pattern tells a story—about family, history, or important lessons. And Sierra Leone? That's part of your great-grandmother, Florene's heritage. She came from the Mende people, who have a strong connection to the Gullah Geechee people in the southeastern United States. They share traditions, history, and culture, especially along the coasts of South Carolina, Georgia, and northern Florida."

For Illustration Purposes Only. A detailed depiction of kente cloth, featuring intricate geometric patterns and bold, vibrant colors like red, gold, green, and blue. The cloth displays traditional West African weaving techniques, displaying a mix of stripes, zigzags, and diamond shapes. The texture appears rich and woven, emphasizing the fabric's cultural significance and artisanship.

Isabella leaned in closer, her eyes studying the map. "And Central Africa?" as she tried to say *'Central'* correctly.

"Yes, Isa, the heart of Africa," Buelo said, his voice full of respect. "In the Congo and Angola regions, the Bantu peoples started a migration that changed the entire continent. They brought with them their knowledge of farming, ironworking, and language—things that are still part of African cultures today. These areas were also at the center of big trade networks, where people shared goods and ideas. And the rhythms they created in their villages? Those rhythms became the foundation of music like jazz, samba, and blues that we listen to today."

For Illustration Purposes Only. A depiction of Angola, showcasing a vibrant mix of its diverse landscapes and culture. The scene depicts an expansive savanna with iconic baobab trees, elephants, and other wildlife. To the right, a view of Luanda, the capital city, with modern high-rise buildings near the coastline, where fishing boats are on the Atlantic Ocean. Also included, locals in traditional dress engaging in dance and music using traditional instruments, set against a backdrop of colorful buildings.

Gabriella leaned against Buelo's arm, her face full of thought. "Do you think they ever imagined us, Buelo?" she asked softly.

Buelo looked at her, his eyes shining with emotion. "Gabby," he said gently, pulling her close, "not only did they imagine us—they dreamed of us. Every bead they strung, every seed they planted, every story they told—they carried us in their hearts, even when things felt impossible."

7 THE MANDINKA AND BALANTA LEGACY

As the warm fire flickered in the family room, Ariella leaned against Buelo, a thoughtful look on her face. "Buelo," she said, "you've told us about your side of the family, but what about Lita's (grandma's)? Where does her family come from?"

Buelo smiled warmly, his eyes shining. "Ah, that's another beautiful part of our story, my loves. Lita's family comes from the Mandinka people of Senegal and the Balanta people of Guinea-Bissau. Both are proud and strong communities with amazing histories."

For Illustration Purposes Only. An artistic depiction of Mandinka people in a traditional setting, featuring men, women, and children engaged in daily activities such as music-making with traditional instruments like the kora (stringed instrument). The Mandinka people are clothed in colorful, intricately patterned traditional attire, including headwraps and jewelry. The setting is a village with round thatched-roof huts, surrounded by greenery and under a bright, sunny sky

Ariella's eyes sparkled with curiosity. "Who are the Mandinka? What were they like?" she asked.

Buelo stroked his beard, thinking. "The Mandinka are one of the largest groups in West Africa. They are known for their amazing oral traditions, shared by griots—storytellers who remember and share history, poetry, and songs passed down through generations. They were part of the Mali Empire, a great kingdom that thrived in the 13th and 14th centuries. Imagine a place full of traders, scholars, and artists, where gold was everywhere, and learning was just as important as treasure."

Gabriella tilted her head thoughtfully. "Did they have kings and queens like other places?" she asked.

Buelo nodded. "Yes, they did! One of the most famous rulers was Mansa Musa, who is known as the richest man in history. He was generous and deeply devoted to his faith, and his actions left a lasting mark on the world. Even though he lived a long time ago, his story reminds us of how brilliant and strong the Mandinka people were."

For Illustration Purposes Only. A depiction of Mansa Musa, the 14th-century Malian emperor, in full regal splendor. He is shown wearing a richly adorned gold robe with elaborate patterns and a jeweled golden crown. In his hand, he holds a golden staff symbolizing his royal authority. Mansa Musa is standing in front of a large map of Africa, signifying his influence on the known world, with piles of gold coins and treasures around him to reflect his legendary wealth. He exudes an aura of wisdom, leadership, and unmatched prosperity.

Isabella chimed in, "What about the Balanta? Were they like the Mandinka?"

Buelo smiled, his voice warm. "The Balanta are very special in their own way. Their name means 'those who resist,' which fits Lita, perfectly. They are known for their independence and strong spirit. Unlike the Mandinka's large kingdoms, the Balanta lived in smaller, close-knit communities. They were amazing farmers, growing rice in the rich lands of Guinea-Bissau. And they believed in fairness—everyone's voice mattered when decisions were made."

Ariella leaned forward, curious. "Did they have special traditions like the Mandinka griots?" she asked.

Buelo chuckled. "Yes, they did. The Balanta have a strong connection to their land and ancestors. Their ceremonies are full of music, dancing, and meaningful symbols. They celebrate the cycles of life, the harvest, and their shared history. They are deeply spiritual, believing in the power of their community and the guidance of their ancestors."

For Illustration Purposes Only. A diverse group of people from Guinea-Bissau, standing outdoors in a vibrant market setting. The group features men, women, and children of various ages, wearing colorful traditional clothing with intricate patterns, including headscarves and wrap skirts. They sell or buy goods like fresh produce and handcrafted items. The background shows small market stalls, local crafts, and a tropical atmosphere with a hint of bright sunshine.

Isabella's voice was soft. "So, now we know where Lita's ancestors came from—the Mandinka and the Balanta!" she roared.

Buelo placed a hand over his heart and smiled. "Yes, my sweet. Lita carries the strength of the Mandinka's great empires and the courage of the Balanta's villages. When you stand tall and speak honestly, you honor them. Their stories, struggles, and victories are part of who we are. When we remember them, we keep them alive, and by sharing their stories, we carry their spirits with us forever."

8 TAKEN: THE PERILOUS JOURNEY TO THE AMERICAS

As the candlelight flickered, casting dancing shadows around the room, Ariella's eyes fell on another map Buelo had placed on the table. It was old, with faded lines and delicate writing, showing a part of West Africa. The title read, *The Slave Coast: Kingdom of Juda.*

"Buelo," Ariella asked, pointing at the map, "I saw something like this in a book at the library. It said this area was called the 'Kingdom of Juda.' Does that mean our family came from here?"

Buelo paused, his face showing both pride and a little sadness as he looked at Ariella. "Ari, you've asked about an important and complicated part of our history. This map," he said, pointing to the coastline, "is a clue that connects our family to the Kingdom of Juda (present-day Republic of Benin), also called Whidah or Whydah on old maps made hundreds of years ago by Europeans."

Credit: Library of Congress, Geography and Map Division. *(Kingdom of Juda, middle-right). Bowen, Emanuel, 1693 Or , Cartographer. A new & accurate map of Negroland and the adjacent countries: also upper Guinea, showing the principle European settlements & distinguishing wch. belong to England, Denmark, Holland & c: the sea of the rivers being drawn from surveys & the best modern maps and charts, & regulated by astron. observns. [London?: Emanuel Bowen, ?, 1747] Map. https://www.loc.gov/item/2018585377/.*

"This region was known for its rich culture and its role in trade—but also for its tragic part in the transatlantic slave trade," Buelo explained.

Gabriella furrowed her brow. "Why was it called the Kingdom of Juda? Does it have anything to do with the Tribe of Judah?" she asked.

Buelo nodded thoughtfully. "That's a good question. Many people believe our ancestors from the Tribe of Judah traveled far and wide, and today, we've found clues like old stories, DNA, and artifacts that connect us to them. These discoveries help us remember who we are, bring back our traditions, and show how important our history is, even if others tried to hide it. It shows how Africans and African descendants have always worked to reclaim their long-lost heritage."

For Illustration Purposes Only. This image portrays the Hebrew Israelites, Tribe of Judah, emphasizing cultural pride and spiritual heritage. The central figure, wrapped in a tallit, symbolizes adherence to Judaic tradition, surrounded by individuals wearing ornate attire blending African and Hebraic elements. The lion signifies strength and royal lineage, while the menorahs highlight faith and continuity. Together, they evoke unity, leadership, and spiritual purpose.

Isabella leaned forward, her voice quiet and sad. "But, Buelo, if they were part of such a strong kingdom, how did they end up being taken?" she asked.

Buelo's face grew serious. "My dear, history can be both inspiring and very painful. The Kingdom of Juda was rich and full of culture, but because it was near the coast, it became a target for European traders. They used local conflicts to turn the area into a center for the transatlantic slave trade. Many of our ancestors were taken from their homes, their families, and their land. But even through such terrible cruelty, they carried their faith, traditions, and strength with them across the ocean. Wherever they went, they planted the seeds of survival."

Ariella looked at the ship's cargo document on the table, her voice steady and full of determination. "So, our story isn't just about loss. It's about strength, isn't it?" she said.

Bassa	10	55	Girl	Naloo	Bissau
Marian	11	55.25	Girl	Mandingo	Bissau
Sarah	9	49.5	Girl	Balanta	Bissau
Ningyeb	9	49	Girl	Naloo	Bissau
Siesah	11	49.5	Girl	Bijogas	Bissau
Teresa	8	49.5	Girl	Bijogas	Bissau
Cumba	9	50	Girl	Mandingo	Bissau
Saville	9	49	Girl	Balanta	Bissau

Buelo placed a hand on Ariella's shoulder, his eyes shining with pride. "That's exactly right, Ari. Our ancestors were so much more than what was done to them," he said warmly.

Gwabannah	29	64	Man	Cromatee	Gold Coast
Gwabana	24	65	Man	Cromatee	Gold Coast
Abannah	25	65	Woman	Cromatee	Gold Coast
Abana	24	62	Woman	Cromatee	Gold Coast
Harfh	7	50	Boy	Cromatee	Gold Coast
Abony	8	50	Boy	Cromatee	Gold Coast
Coffee	12	55.5	Boy	Cromatee	Gold Coast
Abanna	9	51	Girl	Ackoo, Acou, Acc	Gold Coast

"They were creators, builders, and keepers of important traditions," Buelo continued. "Even when they faced the terrible hardships of the slave trade, they found ways to resist, to hold on to who they were, and to pass down their stories."

Onoo	30	70	Man	Robah, Roban	Lagos, Onim
Amoney	30	69	Man	Robah, Roban	Lagos, Onim
Amoney	28	66	Man	Eboo, Hebo	Lagos, Onim
Ober	25	66	Man	Eboo, Hebo	Lagos, Onim
Aacholoo	26	69	Man	Raboli	Lagos, Onim
Ebouk	27	65.5	Man	Eboo, Hebo	Lagos, Onim
Lubbomee	20	67	Man	Raboli	Lagos, Onim

"That's why documents like these are so important," Buelo said gently. "They remind us of our past, but also how far we've come. They connect us to the truth of a people who were once taken to distant shores through the *Door of No Return*."

Gabriella looked at the ship's cargo document from Whydah, her eyes full of curiosity. "Does this mean the Kingdom of Juda is part of us, too?" she asked softly.

Queyah	28	58	Woman	Whydah
Ahsohyee	27	59	Woman	Whydah
Sowayah	26	58	Woman	Whydah
Ahvayway	24	60	Woman	Whydah
Allegaysee	26	61	Woman	Whydah
Ahtaysee	27	64	Woman	Whydah
Ahgussee	30	65	Woman	Whydah

For Illustration Purposes Only. A vibrant depiction of Gullah Geechee people dancing in a lively cultural celebration, set outdoors under the shade of large oak trees draped with Spanish moss. The dancers are dressed in traditional colorful garments, with women wearing headwraps and flowing skirts, and men in shirts with intricate patterns. The scene captures the rhythm of their movement with barefoot dancers stomping on the ground, clapping, and spinning to the beat of drums and traditional music. Other community members are seated in the background, clapping and smiling, enjoying the festive atmosphere, evoking a sense of joy, cultural pride, and history.

Buelo smiled warmly. "Yes, Gabby. It's in the way you sing, the way you dance, and the way you ask questions about the world. It's in the stories I tell you and the ones you'll share with others. The spirit of the Kingdom of Juda, of Whydah, lives in all of us. And as long as we remember, we keep their legacy alive."

The girls sat quietly for a moment, letting Buelo's words sink in. Outside, the wind rustled the leaves, as if carrying whispers from the past. Ariella looked up, her face glowing with a new sense of purpose. "I'll remember, Buelo," she said firmly. "I'll make sure we all remember."

Buelo leaned back, his heart full. "That's all I could ever hope for, Ari. That's all I could ever hope for."

9 CULTURAL RESILIENCE THROUGH THE AFRICAN DIASPORA

Buelo set his cup down on the table, leaned forward, and clasped his hands. After a moment, he looked at the girls and said, "The journey your ancestors took to the Americas, through the hardships of the transatlantic slave trade, shows how incredibly strong and brave they were."

For Illustration Purposes Only. A serene landscape of the Lower Tar-Pamlico River Basin, showcasing the lush wetlands and winding waterways that were home to the Gullah Geechee people, descendants of West African cultures, particularly Sierra Leone. The scene includes towering cypress trees draped with Spanish moss, vibrant green marsh grasses, and a calm, reflective river flowing through the heart of the wetlands. The atmosphere is tranquil, with hints of human history visible through small wooden docks and canoe-like boats tied along the riverbank, symbolizing the connection between the land, water, and the heritage of the Gullah Geechee people.

Buelo's voice became gentle as he said, "Our ancestors were taken from their homes and brought to places like the Lower-Tar Pamlico River Basin, the Western Leeward Islands, and the Georgia Coast. Even in those hard times, they found ways to keep their culture alive and their communities strong. This journey helped shape who African-descended people in the Americas are today."

He paused, his voice quiet and sad. "Our ancestors were treated like property, and their skills were used to build places that didn't belong to them. They worked in fields, growing crops like sugar, rice, and cotton. But even though they faced terrible hardships, they held on to who they were through their culture and traditions, keeping their spirits alive."

Ariella's eyes widened. "Did they sing like we do, Buelo?" she asked.

"Oh, yes," Buelo said with a warm smile. "They sang songs of hope and strength, work songs to cheer themselves up, and spirituals that helped them feel connected to something greater. They also told stories, cooked meals with ingredients from their homeland, and made baskets using skills passed down for generations. These were the ways they held on tight to their identity."

For Illustration Purposes Only. **Left** - *A depiction of a historical plantation setting, focusing on the resilience of African people. The scene features a group of people working in a field with garden tools and baskets, dressed in worn clothing typical of the 19th century. They are singing together, with expressions of solidarity and strength, emphasizing the cultural connection and spirit amidst hardship. The background includes rows of crops and a plantation house visible in the distance, under a semi-cloudy sky.* **Right** - *A depiction of an African American choir singing passionately in a church. The choir members are dressed in elegant choir robes of varying colors, standing in front of stained glass windows casting colorful light into the room. The scene captures the energy, spirituality, and unity of the moment.*

Ariella asked softly, "Does this remind you of what it says in the Bible?"

Buelo smiled at her with pride. "That's a very smart connection, Ari. Many people see how the story of the African diaspora is similar to the passages in Deuteronomy. It's a story about loss, being taken from your home, and wanting to return. But it's also about a promise—a covenant—and about people who worked hard to hold on to who they were, no matter where they went."

As the girls listened, the documents on the table didn't feel as heavy anymore. Instead of symbols of loss, they felt like proof of survival and strength.

For Illustration Purposes Only. An artistic interpretation of Deuteronomy 28:68, symbolizing themes of exile, loss, and resilience. The scene features people from the Kingdom of Juda (Whidah | Whydah) on a shore, gazing solemnly toward large ships on the horizon under a dramatic, stormy sky. They are depicted in culturally significant garments with intricate patterns, reflecting their heritage. Their expressions convey a mixture of sorrow, yet strength. The foreground includes symbolic elements like a withered tree and footprints in the sand leading toward the sea.

10 HONORING ANCESTRY AND HERITAGE

Buelo leaned forward, his voice deep and steady, full of meaning. His eyes moved across the curious faces of Ariella, Gabriella, and Isabella, who sat eagerly, soaking in every word of their family's story. Finally, he asked, "My little lights, **what will you leave for the generations that come after you**?"

For Illustration Purposes Only. Buelo sits in a warm and inviting living room, leaning forward with a gentle and wise expression as he speaks to his three young granddaughters. The room is adorned with cultural symbols, such as African-patterned throws, family photos, and books, creating a cozy and historically rich atmosphere. Warm lighting emphasizes the love and connection in the scene, capturing the gravity of Buelo's words and the girls' youthful determination to carry forward their family's legacy.

Ariella, the oldest, tilted her head, her face thoughtful. "Leave? Like, what kind of things, Buelo? Stories? Lessons?"

Buelo smiled warmly. "Yes, Ari. Stories, lessons, values—even the way you live your life. What you leave behind isn't always something you can touch. It's how you make people feel. It's the example you set. It's the traditions and love you carry forward."

Gabriella nodded slowly. "I want to share our stories, Buelo. All the things you've told us—about Lita's Mandinka and Balanta heritage, about our ancestors in Nigeria and Ghana, and how we came to this country. I don't want anyone to forget where we come from."

For Illustration Purposes Only. Buelo, Lita, and Gabriella in a warm and inviting living room. Gabriella gestures gently while expressing her desire to preserve her family's stories. Lita sits nearby with a supportive and loving gaze. The room is filled with cultural elements like African-patterned textiles, books, and framed photos on the wall, symbolizing their Mandinka and Balanta heritage, as well as connections to Nigeria and Ghana.

Buelo beamed with pride. "That's beautiful, Gabby. The stories of our past help guide our future."

Isabella, her small hands folded in her lap, chimed in. "I think I want to leave kindness. Like, if we're kind and good to people, maybe they'll remember us for that. And then they'll want to be kind, too."

Buelo's eyes glistened as he leaned closer to Isabella. "Kindness is a gift that echoes across generations, Isa. That's a powerful legacy."

For Illustration Purposes Only. Buelo, Lita, and Isabella in a warm and inviting living room. Isabella sits as she looks up with sincerity and innocence. The room is adorned with African-patterned textiles, books, and family photos, symbolizing their heritage and legacy. Warm, soft lighting highlights the intimacy and depth of the moment, capturing the importance of Isabella's words and the family's shared values.

He glanced at Ariella, noticing she frowned slightly, deep in thought. "And you, Ari? What do you think you'll leave?" he asked gently.

Ariella sat up straighter, her voice filled with determination. "I think... strength. Like how our ancestors survived so much and still built amazing things. I want to show future generations that they can be strong, no matter what. And I want to teach them how to stand up for what's right."

For Illustration Purposes Only. Ariella speaking to Buelo in a warm and inviting living room. Ariella sits up straight and her expression full of determination as she speaks about leaving strength as her legacy. Buelo sits across from her, his expression proud and emotional as he listens intently. The room is cozy and culturally rich, adorned with African-patterned textiles, books, and framed family photos that symbolize their heritage. Warm, soft lighting emphasizes the emotional connection and the importance of Ariella's words, capturing the family's values of strength, kindness, and storytelling.

Buelo nodded, his voice full of emotion. "Strength, kindness, stories—all of these are gifts that can guide our family for a long time. What you leave behind doesn't have to be big or perfect. It just has to come from your heart."

The girls sat quietly for a moment, thinking about Buelo's words. They realized it wasn't just a question—it was something much bigger. What they chose to leave behind could shape their family and even the world in the future.

As Buelo gently closed the book and gathered the papers on the table, he looked at them with a warm smile. "My angels, our family's history is like a beautiful quilt, made of many pieces that show how strong and brave our ancestors were. Each part tells a story about people who worked hard, faced challenges, and never gave up. When we remember where we come from, we honor all the amazing things they did. And when we share their stories, we carry their spirit forward for future generations."

For Illustration Purposes Only. A depiction Buelo sitting at a table surrounded by his three granddaughters. Their faces filled with pride and curiosity. The table is adorned with African-patterned textiles, old photographs, and cultural artifacts, symbolizing their rich heritage. The room is warmly lit, creating an intimate and reflective atmosphere that captures the depth of Buelo's words and the legacy he is passing on to his angels.

The end…or, is it?

ABOUT THE AUTHOR

Buelo Addaeyah, a devoted storyteller and passionate historian, brings ancestral tales to life in *The Secret in Our Genes*. Inspired by his own family's journey across continents, Buelo crafts stories that introduce young readers to the power of their heritage. Known to his grandchildren as "Buelo," his tales are infused with a love for the cultures and histories of Africa, and the vibrant peoples who dwell in these lands. Buelo has spent years gathering family stories, tracing genealogies, and exploring ancient histories that reveal the threads connecting his family to the past.

In *The Secret in Our Genes*, he combines this research with his gift for storytelling, presenting children with a world of adventure, discovery, and identity. Through tales of ancestors from the African plains, the Nile's kingdoms, and Israel's tribes, Buelo hopes to instill in readers a sense of belonging and pride in the rich diversity of their roots. When not writing, Buelo travels to historic sites, unearths family mysteries, and, above all, treasures time spent with his granddaughters, whose curious questions and love of learning keep him inspired.

With *The Secret in Our Genes*, Buelo Addaeyah invites families everywhere to explore their own stories and celebrate the powerful connections found in our DNA.

www.ingramcontent.com/pod-product-compliance
Lightning Source LLC
Chambersburg PA
CBRC090917060725
29082CB00003B/8